SPECIAL REPORTS

# CYBERSECURITY

BY MELISSA HIGGINS AND MICHAEL REGAN

CONTENT CONSULTANT
JOSH PAULI, PHD
PROFESSOR
DAKOTA STATE UNIVERSITY

Essential Library
An Imprint of Abdo Publishing | abdopublishing.com

abdopublishing.com

Published by Abdo Publishing, a division of ABDO, PO Box 398166, Minneapolis, Minnesota 55439. 

Printed in the United States of America, North Mankato, Minnesota
082015
012016

THIS BOOK CONTAINS RECYCLED MATERIALS

Cover Photos: Brian A. Jackson/iStockphoto (foreground); Gunnar Assmy/iStockphoto (background)
Interior Photos: Vahid Salemi/AP Images, 5; iStockphoto, 7, 29, 49; Ann Hermes/The Christian Science Monitor/Getty Images, 9; Evan Vucci/AP Images, 13, 91; Bettmann/Corbis, 15, 17; Dave Pickoff/AP Images, 23; Damian Dovarganes/AP Images, 25, 53; Anton Balazh/Shutterstock Images, 27; Ahn Young-joon/AP Images, 32; Shutterstock Images, 35, 59; Martial Trezzini/Keystone/AP Images, 37; J. Scott Applewhite/AP Images, 41; Bryan Bedder/The New Yorker/Getty Images, 45; Brendan Smialowski/AFP/Getty Images, 47; Davor Lovincic/iStockphoto, 56; Jerry Cleveland/The Denver Post/Getty Images, 62; Richard Drew/AP Images, 67; Charles Dharapak/AP Images, 69; Evy Mages/Getty Images, 71; US Navy, 75; John Moore/Getty Images, 79; Scott J. Ferrell/Congressional Quarterly/Getty Images, 81; Rosie Hallam/Express Newspapers/AP Images, 83; Daniel Acker/Bloomberg/Getty Images, 88; Ryan Emberley/Invision for Apple/AP Images, 95; Li Rui/Xinhua News Agency/Newscom, 98

Editor: Arnold Ringstad
Series Designer: Maggie Villaume

Library of Congress Control Number: 2015944931

Cataloging-in-Publication Data

Higgins, Melissa.
Cybersecurity / Melissa Higgins and Michael Regan.
p. cm. -- (Special reports)
ISBN 978-1-62403-899-0 (lib. bdg.)
Includes bibliographical references and index.
1. Computer security--Juvenile literature. 2. Computer crimes--Prevention--Juvenile literature. I. Title. II. Regan, Michael, jt. author.
364.16--dc23

2015944931

# CONTENTS

CHAPTER ONE

# THE WORM THAT CHANGED THE CYBER WORLD

In June 2010, a computer in an Iranian nuclear research laboratory began behaving strangely, restarting itself for no apparent reason. The computer's operators suspected it might be infected with malware, software designed to disrupt computers or steal sensitive information. They hired a Russian company to examine the problem. The company's analysts discovered something disturbing—the biggest, most complex computer attack they had ever seen. On June 17, they sent out a worldwide alert about the malware that would become known as Stuxnet.

The June 2010 cyberattack on an Iranian nuclear research facility brought cybersecurity to international attention.

Symantec, a major US computer security company, took the Stuxnet alert seriously. They dedicated a team of experts to work on the malware around the clock, primarily at the company's malware lab in Culver City, California. Inside the lab, analysts inserted the malware into a simulated network. They discovered Stuxnet was composed of a staggering 15,000 lines of programming code. They estimated it had taken 10,000 hours of work to write this code.[1] Stuxnet was highly sophisticated, taking advantage of four different security holes, known as zero-day vulnerabilities, in the Microsoft Windows operating system.

## ZERO-DAY VULNERABILITY

Software programs and computer hardware sometimes have flaws that are unknown to their developers. These flaws make the software or hardware susceptible to being infiltrated and exploited by hackers. For example, in the case of Stuxnet, hackers found flaws in the Microsoft Windows operating system and used them to install malware. Such flaws are called zero-day vulnerabilities. These are brand-new weaknesses. Their name refers to the idea that there are no days between when a hacker finds a vulnerability and makes his or her first attack. Once developers become aware of a vulnerability, they must quickly fix it by issuing a patch, an updated version of their software that protects against an attack. The result is a race between hackers and developers, with the developer hoping to fix the problem before many users are affected by a hacker's program.

As with security-conscious industries in other parts of the world, the facility in Iran had used a dedicated server—a

Even if a computer is totally isolated from the Internet, it is vulnerable to attacks if the attackers can gain direct physical access.

computer not connected to the Internet—in order to avoid attacks. So how did Stuxnet get in? The analysts believed it may have planted itself on the server after an unsuspecting computer operator plugged in an infected flash drive.

Perhaps the most fascinating and frightening feature of Stuxnet was its behavior. Most malware causes damage that is limited to a computer or a network of computers. But Stuxnet targeted software that operated real-world machines, including pumps, valves, and generators. During the sabotage, the malware instructed the computer to tell workers everything was operating normally.

## WHO CREATED STUXNET, AND WHY?

The Symantec team was able to trace the Stuxnet malware to servers in Malaysia and Denmark. However, this did not necessarily mean it originated in these places. People who carry out cyberattacks often use servers in multiple locations to hide themselves and make it difficult for authorities to trace them. The analysts learned nothing about the perpetrators themselves, but the team was able to determine at least 60 percent of the infections were occurring in Iran.[2] They had been going on since 2009. Ralph Langner, a cybersecurity expert in Hamburg, Germany, ran more experiments with Stuxnet and found evidence the malware was directed at Iran. The likeliest target seemed to be a uranium-enrichment facility in the city of Natanz. Langner determined Stuxnet was designed to make the plant's equipment malfunction and break, with the ultimate goal of slowing Iran's nuclear energy program.

Because of the complexity of the Stuxnet coding, and the specific knowledge required to make it, many investigators—including Symantec and

Langner—believed its creators must have been supported by a government. Since Israel and the United States believed Iran was trying to build nuclear weapons and should be prevented from doing so, these two nations were the primary suspects. While the two countries have not confirmed their involvement, investigative journalists and researchers have found evidence the two nations, working together, were likely behind the attack.

New infections of Stuxnet are rare now, because soon after learning about Stuxnet in June 2010, Microsoft fixed the holes in Windows the malware had used. Still, the malware had brought a new threat to the world of cybersecurity. Stuxnet proved an individual, group, or

In his work as a cybersecurity consultant, Langner works to defend infrastructure and manufacturing facilities.

nation could attack a country's water, energy, or other infrastructure systems using a cyberweapon. The danger from malware was no longer simply virtual. Real-world systems using computers, such as nuclear power plants, energy grids, and water supplies, were recognized as vulnerable.

## NOT NEW, BUT A GROWING PROBLEM

While Stuxnet may have marked the beginning of a new, more dangerous era of cyberthreats, cybersecurity has been an issue since the earliest days of the Internet. Today, computers heat water, brew coffee, run manufacturing plants, and operate cars, planes, trains, and phones. Computers are not only everywhere, but are also interconnected. The first e-mail was sent in 1971. Today,

### MALICIOUS SOFTWARE TERMS

There are many types of malware. Adware displays unwanted advertisements. Ransomware locks away a user's data and demands money in exchange for releasing it. Spyware tracks a user's online activity and transmits it to a third party. A Trojan horse comes bundled with seemingly legitimate software and activates when that software is installed on a computer. A virus spreads through downloaded e-mails and Internet files, attaching itself to existing programs. It is often designed to cause damage by deleting files or using up memory. A worm operates on its own, rather than through a separate program. It makes copies of itself to infect other computers. Stuxnet is an example of a worm.

40 trillion e-mails are sent every year. When the first website was unveiled in 1991, its creator did not anticipate that by 2013 there would be more than 30 trillion web pages.[3]

"WHEN I STARTED IN MY CAREER, IN THE LATE EIGHTIES, IF THERE WAS A BANK ROBBERY, THE POOL OF SUSPECTS WAS LIMITED TO THE PEOPLE WHO WERE IN THE VICINITY AT THE TIME. NOW WHEN A BANK IS ROBBED THE POOL OF SUSPECTS IS LIMITED TO THE NUMBER OF PEOPLE IN THE WORLD WITH ACCESS TO A FIVE-HUNDRED-DOLLAR LAPTOP AND AN INTERNET CONNECTION."[6]

**—SHAWN HENRY, FORMER EXECUTIVE ASSISTANT DIRECTOR OF THE FBI'S CYBER DIVISION**

A downside to all of this connectivity is that networks can be attacked by anyone with a motive and the knowledge of how to do so. Many of the largest companies in the United States have been hacked. In 2010, the cybersecurity firm McAfee discovered a new piece of malware every 15 minutes. Only three years later, in 2013, it was finding one every second.[4]

In 2009, US President Barack Obama said, "It's the great irony of our Information Age—the very technologies that empower us to create and to build also empower those who would disrupt and destroy. . . . Cyber threat is one of the most serious economic and national security challenges we face as a nation."[5] The *Boston Globe* newspaper declared in 2009 that a "cyber world war" was already in progress.[7] The increase in the number and severity of cyberthreats has resulted in a booming business for cybersecurity firms and the creation of new government offices and military units to deal with them.

For individual users, cyberthreats create a sense of vulnerability. Gone are the days when Internet users' only security headaches were downloading computer viruses that might slow down their computers or draw smiley faces on their screens. Today, they must worry about thieves stealing their credit card numbers, their bank account information, and even their identities. A type of malware known as spyware can track a user's online activity and send that information to corporations or even government agencies.

## NO EASY SOLUTIONS

Cybersecurity is a relatively new, technically complex issue. As a result, it is often poorly understood by government officials, corporate leaders, and the public at large. Discovering the identity of cybercriminals can frustrate law enforcement when sophisticated perpetrators route their online activity through servers located all around the world. While most people agree cybercrime is a problem, there is no consensus on just how severe it is. There is also little agreement on the best ways to fight it, and current solutions are far from perfect. One thing on which many cybersecurity experts agree is that humans are the weakest link in the cybersecurity equation. This means the more the public understands about how their computers and networks work, the better equipped they will be to protect themselves from cybercrimes.

In early 2015, President Obama spoke about cybersecurity, highlighting its importance as a part of the country's overall national security.

CHAPTER TWO

# INTERNET HISTORY

During the Industrial Revolution, the steam engine allowed workers to manufacture goods faster and more easily than ever before. In the modern information age, the computer is making calculations easier and faster, enabling people to solve problems and carry out tasks. The first computers were big and slow, but they calculated and stored data better than any single person could. It was not long before scientists realized the potential of connecting multiple computers together. Their efforts led to the first computer networks. Eventually, networks were connected to other networks, forming vast groups of interconnected computers. Computer experts soon

Early computers filled entire rooms.

discovered they could exploit these networks for both personal fun and illegal gains.

## THE FIRST COMPUTERS AND NETWORKS

Charles Babbage, a professor at Cambridge University in the United Kingdom, designed an ingenious mechanical computer in 1837. The enormous machine, known as an analytical engine, would use gears and other moving parts to carry out calculations and solve problems. However, it was never built during his lifetime. The successors to Babbage's designs, the first computers that used electric switches rather than mechanical gears, were not invented until the mid-1900s.

As with many inventions, the computer got a big boost in its infancy from the military. In 1943, the US military commissioned the first general-purpose electronic computer during World War II (1939–1945). It was to be used for computing weapons trajectories, enabling the military to lob explosive shells more accurately. Military officials hoped the machine, known as the electronic numerical integrator and computer (ENIAC), would be capable of computing 100 times faster than a person using

Programmers used ENIAC by manipulating a large bank of switches and dials.

traditional methods. In the end, ENIAC proved capable of computing 300,000 times faster than a person.[1]

In 1958, President Dwight D. Eisenhower created the Advanced Research Projects Agency (ARPA) to support and promote technological research. ARPA had the goal of making sure the United States did not fall behind the Soviet Union in technological advancements. In 1968, leaders from ARPA enlisted engineers from three private companies to create a network of computers that could share data and boost computing power. A big hurdle the engineers faced was that the four computers they hoped to connect all used different operating systems. That meant the engineers would have to write 12 different software programs so each computer could send and receive data with each of the three other computers.

However, the engineers came up with a simpler solution. Each participant in the test was given a computer known as an interface message processor (IMP). The IMPs were connected to each other by dedicated long-distance telephone lines so they could transmit data between each other. The IMP on the receiving end would translate the information for its user's main computer. In this way, engineers had to write only four programs—ones that connected each main computer with its IMP. The connected computers were called the ARPANET.

## THE INTERNET AND THE WORLD WIDE WEB

The first ARPANET was set up in 1969. It connected computers located at the University of California, Los

Angeles (UCLA); the Stanford Research Institute; the University of California, Santa Barbara; and the University of Utah. By 1972, the ARPANET had dozens of participants, including consulting firms, government and military sites, and universities. Other organizations besides ARPA began building their own networks, but none of the networks were connected to each other. In 1976, after three years of work, engineers connected the ARPANET to another network called the packet radio network (PRNET) using radio transmitters and receivers instead of phone lines. The satellite network (SATNET) joined in 1977, and this network of networks became known as the Internet. The

"[ARPANET] CAME OUT OF OUR FRUSTRATION THAT THERE WERE ONLY A LIMITED NUMBER OF LARGE, POWERFUL RESEARCH COMPUTERS IN THE COUNTRY AND THAT MANY RESEARCH INVESTIGATORS WHO SHOULD HAVE ACCESS WERE GEOGRAPHICALLY SEPARATED FROM THEM."[2]

**—CHARLES M. HERZFELD, FORMER DIRECTOR OF ARPA**

## *LO*

In their first attempt at communication using the ARPANET, researchers at UCLA tried to log on to a computer at the Stanford Research Institute. But before they could type the letter *g* in *login*, the Stanford computer crashed. All that got through was *lo*. This was the first word transmitted over a computer network.

original Internet was not designed to be widely available, so few safeguards were added to the design.

The Internet at this point already contained vast amounts of data, and users had a difficult time searching for and finding what they needed. In 1990, Tim Berners-Lee, a software engineer at a research center in Switzerland, created hypertext markup language (HTML), a computer language used to make web pages. He also developed the protocols for uniform resource identifiers (URIs)—which tell the name and location of files on the web—and the hypertext transfer protocol (HTTP)—a set of rules for transferring files. These new technologies made navigating the Internet easier. Hypertext documents made up the earliest versions of the World Wide Web. They still form the core of most websites today.

## THE FIRST PERSONAL COMPUTERS

The first personal computers were introduced in 1975. The MITS Altair 8800 was sold as a kit the buyer had to assemble. The Apple I, first sold in 1976, was also a kit computer. Users needed to add a keyboard and power supply to use it.

Web browsers, software for navigating the World Wide Web, were in widespread use by 1993. By 1994, businesses were looking for ways to advertise and sell their products on the web. In 1995, companies such as Compuserve, America Online, and Prodigy began offering consumers access to the web and e-mail services. That same year, the online stores Amazon.com and eBay started operations.

### HYPERTEXT

The term *hypertext* dates to the 1960s. It is used to describe text that contains hyperlinks—links, for short. Links are clickable areas of text that bring the user to related content on a different page. Hypertext came into widespread use in the 1990s, when it was used as the primary navigation system on the World Wide Web.

## HACKERS AND PHREAKS

In the 1960s, computer security consisted of locking the door to the computer room and making sure the key was safe. In the mid-1970s, early personal computers rarely connected to each other. Yet even amid that relative security, computers were not immune from being hacked. Rather than acting maliciously, early hackers tended to be expert software programmers. They attempted to "hack" out clever solutions to problems with their computer software. They sought to make computers work faster, complete new tasks, or simply gain a better understanding of how software worked.

The ARPANET was also relatively secure because it used dedicated communications lines and could only be accessed by someone using one of the networked computers. Still, some curious and dedicated hackers managed to break into the network.

During the 1970s, a less noble form of hacking, called phreaking, developed. Phreakers hacked electronic telephone switching systems. By playing certain sound frequencies into public telephones, they could make free phone calls. Some of the most influential visionaries and hackers in the computer world got their start in this illegal practice, including the cofounders of Apple Computer, Steve Jobs and Steve Wozniak. The pair sold phone phreaking equipment, known as blue boxes, when they were in college.

## CYBERCRIME

A turning point in the history of hacking occurred with the proliferation of personal computers during the 1980s. Practically anyone could buy a computer for his or her own use. These computers, along with devices called modems that enabled computers to communicate with each other over telephone wires, extended the reach of hackers. It was during this time that some hackers decided to use their skills for criminal purposes. They copied and distributed commercial software and games. A few hackers unleashed viruses capable of shutting down computers and entire network systems. To differentiate themselves

Among the most notorious phreakers was John Draper, who received the nickname "Captain Crunch" after hacking a telephone switching system using a toy whistle from a cereal box.

from these malicious coders, legal hackers began referring to themselves as white-hat hackers. Malicious hackers became known as black-hat hackers. Today, the term *hacker* is commonly used in association with malicious activity. However, computer experts typically use *hacker* to describe anyone who seeks flaws in software that can be exploited, whether for good or bad purposes.

Cybersecurity threats increased with the birth of the web. In the mid-1990s, several arrests of high-profile hackers proved the seriousness with which law enforcement now took malicious hacking. Kevin Mitnick, one of the best-known black-hat hackers, spent five years in prison for his cyber-related crimes and was barred from using computers for several years after getting out of jail. He later became a successful white-hat

## THE LEGALITY OF HACKING

Until the mid-1980s, criminal hacking was not technically illegal. Stealing computer software and games was illegal, but hacking into a computer system was not. Legislators and law enforcement agencies, pressured by hacked businesses and government agencies, began proceedings to criminalize and prosecute these activities. In 1986, the US Congress passed the federal Computer Fraud and Abuse Act. It made computer tampering a felony crime. Perpetrators could be punished with jail time and fines.

Black-hat hacker Kevin Mitnick, *right*, was released from prison in January 2000.

hacker, showing businesses how to improve their computer security.

A generation ago, the Internet linked a handful of computers around the world. In the 2010s, it is an integral part of billions of people's lives. With such a rapid development and spread, it is not surprising problems have arisen. The devices and protocols that make up the Internet have made the modern interconnected world possible, but they have also proved vulnerable to malicious hackers.

CHAPTER THREE

# HOW IT ALL WORKS

The Internet is no longer confined to closed networks transferring scientific data from one university to another. Vital infrastructure is operated using the Internet. Governments store important data online. Every day people bank, buy products, and share details about their lives online. As individuals, corporations, and governments rely more and more on the Internet, they become even more vulnerable to cyberattacks. To understand how these attacks happen, it is important to understand how the modern Internet works.

The modern Internet is a vast network of networks that spans the globe.

## PACKETS AND PROTOCOLS

The Internet consists of two parts: hardware and protocols. Hardware includes the physical parts that make up the Internet, such as cables, personal computers, and smartphones. Routers, devices that join networks together, and servers, computers that manage access to networks, are critical components. Protocols are rules that tell the hardware how to direct and use the information being transmitted. This common set of rules makes it possible for a wide assortment of different hardware devices to communicate with each other.

Information moves between these devices quickly, but it goes through many steps along the way. Imagine a person takes a smartphone photo of a cat and wants to send it to her friend's smartphone. When she hits send, the protocol instructions break the picture up into many individual pieces called packets. In addition to a tiny part of the original photo, each packet includes information about where it came from and where it is going. It also carries instructions about how to correctly reassemble the photo once the packets arrive at their destination.

The packets are sent separately over the Internet through routers. Each router reads the packet's origin and destination and determines where the packet should go next. The packets jump from router to router through fiber-optic cables, satellites, radio waves, or telephone lines, until they reach the friend's phone. The phone puts the picture back together and shows the photo on its screen. The entire process takes seconds or less. The packet-using protocol is known as the Internet protocol (IP).

One of the strengths of the Internet is that there are many different routes a packet can take. If one route breaks down for some reason, the packet can be redirected along a different route and still reach its

Devices called routers and switches move packets to their destinations.

destination. In fact, most packets do not take the same route. This process works well for most Internet activities, such as sending and receiving e-mails or tweets. However, the process does not work as well for streaming media, such as videos and music. Streaming media still gets broken into packets, but the packets are sent in order along the same route so the movie or music can play smoothly at its destination.

## WHY IS THE INTERNET VULNERABLE?

One reason the Internet is vulnerable to hacking lies in its original design. It is an open system encouraging universal access. The technologies and software making up the Internet are open source. This means the programming code used to make them can be read by anyone. People can study the technology, learn how it works, and use it to their advantage.

Another issue is the architecture of the web. When opening a web page, the files that make up the page, including text, images, and small programs, are downloaded to the user's computer. If a hacker has tampered with any of these files, they can become doorways for cybercriminals to plant malware or carry out other attacks.

To prevent cyberattacks, many businesses and individuals use firewalls. This combination of specialized software and hardware tries to screen out hacking attempts and malware, protecting the user from potential attacks. Many operating systems now have firewalls built in. When a computer is considered unimportant or insignificant, sometimes users do not bother with firewalls. But a network is only as strong as its weakest link. Once cybercriminals have made their way into an unprotected computer, it may become much easier for them to spread through the entire network.

## BOTNETS

A botnet is a network of hijacked computers controlled by a hacker used to quickly distribute malware, steal data, or carry out other cybercrimes. Botnets can range in size from dozens of computers to hundreds of thousands. The computers' owners may not even know their machines are participating in a botnet. Slowdowns, crashes, and mysterious messages may be clues that a computer belongs to a botnet. Victim machines are often called zombie computers, and the hackers who control them are known as bot herders or botmasters. Hackers operate their botnets from afar using software known as remote administration tools, or RATs.

Many nations that deal with cyber threats, including South Korea, now have dedicated antihacking teams.

## THE MAJOR PLAYERS AND WHAT THEY WANT

In the early 2000s, many hackers planted viruses and other malware mainly for the challenge and sport of it. Today, the major players in the world of cybercrime are criminals and governments. Cybercriminals seek to make money from both individuals and corporations. They sometimes use a technique called phishing, which involves directing a large number of users to a trustworthy-looking website, hoping some of them will fall for the trick and provide sensitive information. Or they might target a specific person with a similar personalized message. This directed approach is called spear phishing. Hardware, including flash drives, DVDs, and microchips, can also be infected with malware.

Governments use similar techniques to gain access to computer systems, although their goals are not the same as those of cybercriminals. Rather than money, they seek to steal state and defense secrets, spy on people, or interfere with another country's military operations. They might want to destabilize a foreign country by disrupting utilities or transportation. Whatever the goals, hackers first need to gain access to the systems they want to infiltrate. State-sponsored cyberespionage has become a common phenomenon in the 2010s.

## CAN AN ELECTION BE HACKED?

With the advent of electronic voting, some cybersecurity experts worry elections can too easily be rigged. Prior to the 2012 US presidential election, computer vulnerability specialist Roger Johnston demonstrated he could hack into two voting machines—the touchscreen Diebold Accuvote-TSX and the push-button Sequoia AVC—and change voting results. Combined, these types of machines were used by 35 million voters in 24 states.[1] Voting machines could also contain software bugs or election-rigging malware. Some states have stopped using their voting systems because of hacking vulnerabilities. Federal standards for voting machines have not been updated since 2005, so there has been little incentive for voting machine manufacturers to upgrade to new technology.

# FROM THE HEADLINES

## MALADVERTISING

Sometimes Internet providers and websites place advertising onto their web pages as a way to make money. At other times, website operators have no intention of displaying ads, but malware programs inject ads where they are not intended. These forced ads sometimes sell real products, but they can also introduce even more malware. From the end of 2014 to the beginning of January 2015, a number of major websites, including *The Huffington Post* and Internet service provider America Online (AOL), displayed advertisements laced with a malware program called Kovter. The malware infected computers, locked them down, and showed a fake message from the Federal Bureau of Investigation (FBI) asking for money. Victims did not even have to click on the offending ad. As soon as it appeared onscreen, it infected vulnerable computers.

The incident demonstrates how difficult it is to catch maladvertising and how prevalent it is becoming. The perpetrators behind Kovter redirected the source of the ads several times, making themselves difficult to track and identify. Investigators for AOL eventually traced the source website to a server in Poland. Security researcher Nick Bilogorskiy noted the malware targeted every visitor to HuffingtonPost.com before it was removed. "These

Internet advertising brings in billions of dollars each year for major companies, including search engine giant Google.

criminals really turned up the exposure and tried to compromise lots of people," he said in an interview. "It's unprecedented. We've never seen it at this scale."[2] Because the Kovter malware blocked access to files rather then encrypting them, users could restore access by rebooting their computers in safe mode, and then using antivirus software to remove the malware. As of January 2015, the Kovter criminals had not been caught and were still actively planting the malware on various websites.

CHAPTER FOUR

# HACKERS AND HACKTIVISTS

In the early days of the Internet, hackers were often computer enthusiasts more interested in learning about computer networks and testing their skills than in stealing things. Many still operate this way in the 2010s. But another type of hacker has emerged. These hackers use their skills to carry out cybercrimes. Some act alone. Others join small groups. Large organized gangs of hackers have also formed. Who are hackers, and what motivates them?

## WHITE HATS

In the early days of the Internet, many hackers participated in bulletin boards, sharing their hacking

Australian hacker Julian Assange later became an activist when he cofounded WikiLeaks, an organization that releases classified information.

exploits and trying to outdo each other by breaking into the most secure websites they could find. This kind of sharing among hackers is still done.

In addition to hacking as a hobby, white-hat hackers are hired by a variety of employers, including cybersecurity companies, corporations, and governments. Hackers use their knowledge and skill to write security software and make existing software more secure. An assignment often requested by corporate clients is attack and penetration, called attack and pen for short. Hackers break into a client's computer to find weaknesses and then suggest ways the weaknesses can be fixed. Government hacking jobs are more secretive. They may involve attacking terrorist networks, penetrating organized crime groups, or finding foreign cybercriminals.

## HACKER CONVENTIONS

Every year, hackers gather for DEF CON and Black Hat, two US hacker conferences held during the same week in the same place, with slightly difference audiences. DEF CON is a conference "by hackers, for hackers," and features contests to see who can break passwords or hack into a system the fastest. Black Hat is more educational and technical in scope, with presentations on research projects and classes on security techniques. It attracts computer security professionals from both the public and private sectors. Hundreds of hacker conventions now take place around the world.

# MORE TO THE STORY

## HIGH DEMAND FOR HACKERS

The demand for talented hackers is intense, as is the competition to hire them. When it wants to hire hackers, the US government must compete with private security firms, which can offer six-figure salaries to candidates. Private hacking work also comes with fewer hassles. For example, as part of an FBI background check, candidates cannot be hired if they have used drugs more than a handful of times. "That disqualifies a bunch of people that would be perfectly skilled and trustworthy, just because they smoked pot in college," Jeff Moss, founder of the DEF CON hacker convention, told a reporter.[1] The National Security Agency (NSA) offered one candidate a job after he graduated from college, promising him a large salary and a company car. But he turned down the offer because of the federal security check that would be required.

Hackers tend to be creative thinkers who do not fit well into government bureaucracies that expect employees to conform to rules and regulations. The government is trying to improve this image to attract hackers. While government hackers are not allowed to work at home, the hours are flexible, and men are not required to wear suits and ties. Hackers may be attracted to government jobs since they get to work on missions not available to other professionals. Others may be interested in government positions because they want to protect their country. As of 2012, federal cybersecurity professionals earned up to $155,000 per year.[2]

## BLACK-HAT HACKERS AND SCRIPT KIDDIES

While white-hat hackers work to protect software and hardware, black-hat hackers do whatever they can to get around cybersecurity measures. They are motivated by profit, a political cause, or general maliciousness. They leave viruses, steal credit card numbers, shut down networks, destroy files, and collect victims' personal information to sell.

Talented black-hat hackers can earn six-figure incomes hacking to gain intelligence or carry out sabotage. Some black hats make money by discovering vulnerabilities in software programs and then selling that information. Others demand software or hardware companies pay a ransom for the information. Companies have sprung up that sell vulnerability information to affected companies or to anyone who wants to exploit these holes.

### FREELANCE HACKERS FOR HIRE

Some hackers make their services available online for a price. This allows someone without computer expertise to hire an expert to do the work for them. People post assignments and take bids from freelance hackers. These workers can be used for malicious purposes, but there are also many legal jobs the hackers can do. A company may hire a freelance hacker to test its computer defenses against threats.

The US government hires hackers to counter individuals, groups, and governments that target US computers.

Malicious hackers do not need to be talented to make money from the Internet. Many rely on a variety of ready-made programs that break into networks, create botnets, crack passwords, and phish. These programs are created by talented hackers and are sold or given away online. The relatively unskilled hackers who use these programs are dismissively named "script kiddies" or "packet monkeys."[3] They may not even know how to write programs themselves or how the programs they are using really work. They may have simply watched an online video on how to get started. Cybersecurity experts believe there may be millions of these hackers on the Internet today.

## DIFFERENT HATS

There are other hacker nicknames besides white hats and black hats. Hackers working for Microsoft to find vulnerabilities in Windows are known as blue hats. Hackers who work on both legal and illegal projects are known as gray hats. The original terms *black hat* and *white hat* came from old western movies, in which the bad guys usually wore black hats and the good guys wore white.

## HACKTIVISTS

Another type of hacker, the hacktivist—short for hacker activist—uses computers and computer networks to promote a political cause. Perhaps the best-known hacktivist group is Anonymous. With members spread out across the world, this group focuses on attacking institutions and promoting political causes while its members retain their anonymity. In 2008, the group began hitting the Church of Scientology with denial-of-service attacks, a technique that overloads a target server and causes it to shut down. In 2010, Anonymous struck PayPal and credit card companies with more denial-of-service attacks when they refused to process payments to

WikiLeaks, an organization that releases secret government and corporate documents. Other organizations also undertake hacktivist causes. In 2011, during the political uprising known as the Arab Spring, the Egyptian government tried to shut down Internet service within the country to prevent dissenters from organizing. A movement called Speak2Tweet allowed people inside Egypt to leave messages on Twitter using telephones.

## DENIAL-OF-SERVICE ATTACKS

Hacktivists sometimes use denial-of-service (DoS) attacks to get their political messages across. In a DoS attack, hackers repeatedly access a particular website, overloading the site's servers and causing them to slow down or freeze. Another version of DoS is the distributed denial-of-service attack, or DDoS. The goal is the same as with a DoS—to overload and shut down a network—but the attackers use many computers. This makes the work easier and faster. In addition to hacktivists, cyberterrorists and cybercriminals use DoS attacks to threaten national security by shutting down access to banks, governments, the media, or vital infrastructure.

Another type of hacktivist is the cyber whistleblower, a person who uses technical skills and a position inside government or industry to expose what they consider unethical or illegal behavior. Two of the best-known cyber whistleblowers are Chelsea Manning—previously known as Bradley Manning—and Edward Snowden. On May 27, 2010, the US military arrested US Army private

Bradley Manning for leaking videos from the wars in Iraq and Afghanistan, along with approximately 250,000 classified US diplomatic messages.[4] Manning's job in military intelligence gave him access to classified computer networks. He believed the information he saw should be made public. He downloaded the files and passed them on to WikiLeaks. Manning was given a 35-year prison sentence in 2013.

Edward Snowden, an employee of a government contractor, had access to top-secret National Security Agency (NSA) and Central Intelligence Agency (CIA) documents during his employment. Over time, Snowden became disenchanted with the government's surveillance programs. He believed the government was illegally spying on US citizens. Snowden copied more than 60,000 classified documents onto flash drives and distributed them to several journalists in 2013.[5] Unlike Manning, Snowden was not caught. He fled to Russia, where he was living in exile in 2015.

Whether hacktivists like Manning and Snowden are heroes or villains depends on one's perspective. Many consider them traitors for illegally exposing government secrets. Others believe they have provided a valuable service to their country for bringing examples of government wrongdoing to light.

Since moving to Russia, Snowden has given interviews to US journalists over Internet video.

CHAPTER FIVE

# THREATS TO COMPANIES

Corporations—especially banks and online stores—provide a treasure trove of online data for criminal hackers, including credit card and bank account numbers. Defense companies are also common targets for cyberattacks, whether hackers are working on behalf of a rival company or a foreign military. Solving cybercrimes against corporations becomes complicated when the lines of responsibility blur between private and national security and when companies fail to report cyberattacks.

In early 2015, US law enforcement announced a $3 million reward for helping track down a hacker who had stolen more than $100 million from banks across the world.

WANTED
BY THE FBI

## THE TARGET BREACH

Before Thanksgiving 2013, cybercriminals based in Odessa, Ukraine, hacked into the computer network of the retail giant Target. Once inside the network, the hackers planted malware designed to steal customers' credit card numbers from all US Target stores. Six months prior to the attack, Target had prepared itself for just such an event, spending $1.6 million on a state-of-the-art malware detection tool.[1] The tool worked perfectly. On November 30 and again on December 2, 2013, the detection software alerted Target security-system monitors about a possible attack. However, the personnel at Target's security operations center did not respond to the threat. By December 15, 2013, 40 million credit and debit card numbers were stolen.[2] In the wake of the attack, Target's stock price and earnings saw severe downturns.

### TARGET ATTACKERS TARGETED

The website set up by the hackers to sell Target credit card data was hacked itself in March 2014. The unknown hackers—possibly vigilantes or competitors wanting to shut down the operation—stole the usernames, passwords, and payment information of those buying the stolen data and posted the data online.

Because Target failed to protect its customers' credit

The Target hack put the personal information of millions of shoppers at risk.

card data, in March 2015, a federal judge approved a $10 million lawsuit brought by customers of Target.[3] Shortly after Target announced the security breach in 2014, officials from the retailer said they would be spending more than $100 million for new registers that would read secure credit cards using embedded chips rather than more vulnerable magnetic strips.[4]

The Target data breach was the largest hack against a US retailer at that time. It cost the company hundreds of millions of dollars and shook consumer confidence in credit card purchases. It also demonstrated how much damage a few cybercriminals could cause using simple hacking techniques.

## THE SONY ATTACK

In 2014, two corporate cyberbreaches demonstrated how the lines between private and national interests could blur. In November, computers at Sony Pictures were hacked shortly before the entertainment company planned to release the movie *The Interview*, a comedy with a plot about assassinating the North Korean leader, Kim Jong-un. The cyberattack—which destroyed data, stole social security numbers, leaked confidential e-mails, and caused $100 million in damage—was thought to be carried out by the North Korean government to keep the movie out of theaters.[5] Fearing more attacks, and amid threats of physical attacks on theaters, Sony canceled the film's release after major theater companies declined to show the film. A widespread outcry that the film's cancellation was an affront to free speech led Sony to release the film in a few theaters and make it available online. Computer forensics specialists traced the attack to a hacking firm called DarkSeoul, working on behalf of the North Korean government.

In February 2014, Las Vegas Sands Corporation, the parent company of three Las Vegas casinos, was hacked after the company's owner, Sheldon Adelson, gave a speech calling for a nuclear attack on Iran. The cyberattack wiped out his company's computer servers, causing $40 million in damage.[6] A cybersecurity firm hired by Adelson concluded the attack originated in Iran. The targets of these two cyberattacks were corporations, but the attackers allegedly acted on behalf of foreign governments. As a result, the public, politicians, and security experts debate whether the US government should retaliate in some way for these attacks and others like them.

## SURPRISINGLY VULNERABLE

A casino in Minnesota hired Accuvant, a cybersecurity company, to find the weaknesses in their security systems and fix them. As part of the test, casino employees were not informed about Accuvant's presence. An Accuvant security team convinced workers they were tech support staff, walked away with the casino's servers, and piled them next to the casino's slot machines. The photo they took of themselves posing with the equipment convinced the casino's management that security needed to be improved.

# FROM THE HEADLINES

## THE US RESPONSE TO THE SONY ATTACK

In December 2014, shortly after the serious cyberattack against Sony Pictures, North Korea experienced a temporary shutdown of the Internet. US officials declined to confirm whether the United States was behind the cyberattack against North Korea, although at a press conference, homeland security official Lisa Monaco said, "The US government takes [the Sony hack] very, very seriously and will address it as such."[7] The United States eventually took legal action. On January 2, 2015, the Obama administration imposed economic sanctions against several North Korean officials and government agencies, blaming the country for "provocative, destabilizing, and repressive actions and policies, particularly its destructive and coercive cyber attack on Sony Pictures Entertainment."[8]

The leveling of sanctions against North Korea was the first time the US government had retaliated for a cyberattack against a private company, a decision made after a meeting of top officials in the White House Situation Room on December 17, 2014. Admiral Michael S. Rogers, director of the NSA, said in an interview about the meeting, "The argument I made was the whole

The hack of Sony Pictures led to a major international dispute.

world is watching how we as a nation respond. And if we don't acknowledge this, if we don't name names here, it will only . . . encourage others to decide, 'Well, this must not be a red line for the United States. This must be something they're comfortable [with] and willing to accept.'"[9]

## ISSUES WITH GOVERNMENT INTERVENTION

Some cybersecurity experts believe the US government should intervene on behalf of private companies, depending on the seriousness of the attack. For example, if one bank gets hacked, that should remain the bank's problem. But if a dozen banks are hacked by the same organization, it might become an issue of national security. It is not clear who decides when a hack has crossed that line. The US government provides Information Sharing and Analysis Centers (ISACs) to help businesses secure their computers and networks. Participation is voluntary, and many private companies prefer to avoid subjecting themselves to government regulations with mandatory security requirements.

Another problem with government involvement is the difficulty of identifying the perpetrator. Tracking the source of a cyberattack is not always a sure thing, and a US president might be disinclined to retaliate against a foreign government without definitive proof of that government's involvement. For example, evidence arose that the hack against Sony may have actually been an inside job by a disgruntled former employee, although the FBI strongly disputes that conclusion.

## RELUCTANCE TO REPORT

Another factor complicating corporate cyberthreats is the reluctance of companies to report attacks once they've happened. After his Las Vegas company was hacked, Sheldon Adelson hired a cybersecurity company to trace the intrusion. Before the details of the report were made public in an article in *Bloomberg Businessweek*, Adelson tried to cover up the scope and nature of the attack.

The reasons companies fail to report hacking incidents are varied, but they mostly boil

### OTHER CORPORATE HACKS

In addition to Sony and Target, other major US companies have been targeted by cyberattacks in recent years:

2000: Yahoo! and eBay suffered large-scale denial-of-service attacks.

2006: The personal information of 650,000 AOL users was posted publicly.[10]

2007: 94 million credit cards of T. J. Maxx shoppers were exposed.[11]

2008: 134 million credit cards belonging to users of Heartland Payment Systems were exposed.[12]

2009: Intellectual property was stolen from technology giants Yahoo! and Google.

2011: 77 million accounts on Sony's PlayStation Network were hacked.[13]

2014: Checking and savings account information belonging to customers of J. P. Morgan Chase and other banks was exposed.

2014: 56 million user accounts from Home Depot were accessed.[14]

2015: 14 million member records from Anthem health insurance were accessed.[15]

The huge amounts of money that move through casinos make them major targets for hackers.

down to profit. Retail businesses worry customers will lose trust in their company and spend their dollars elsewhere. This played out after the Target breach in November 2013, after which the retailer saw a 5.3 percent drop in sales over the previous year.[16] Companies also worry stock prices will decline, and that the cybersecurity measures they will need to put into place after a breach are too expensive. Further, companies worry that revealing hacks will force them to publicly disclose security vulnerabilities that might put them at risk for future attacks.

In 2002, the California legislature passed a law requiring companies to report if hackers compromised customer data. In 2004, the year before the law took effect, three companies announced cybersecurity breaches. A year later, 51 companies reported breaches. As of 2013, similar laws were in effect in 46 states. Even so, companies are still reluctant to deal with cyberattacks. A 2011 study found half of the 1,000 companies surveyed did not investigate a security breach.[17]

Businesses are high-value targets, but they are not the only victims of cybercriminals. Individuals' computers and personal electronic devices are also prime targets for hackers.

## THE COST OF CORPORATE CYBERCRIME

The cost of cybercrime is high. It is estimated to cost the global economy $445 billion a year, according to a 2014 report by the software security firm McAfee.[18] In the United States in 2013, companies with more than 1,000 employees spent an average of $9 million a year on cybersecurity.[19] Although news reports tend to focus on cyberattacks against large, high-profile companies, a 2014 study by a cybersecurity research firm found smaller companies are more at risk for cyberattacks because they are less likely to use strong cybersecurity measures.

CHAPTER SIX

# THREATS TO PERSONAL COMPUTERS

The tools cybercriminals use against individuals are very similar to the ones they use against businesses, consisting of malware planted through phishing scams or infected files or websites. While companies offer larger troves of data to steal, individuals make easier targets because most people do not have the resources or knowledge to keep themselves and their data secure, even if they are aware it is important to do so. A survey by the National Cyber Security Alliance released in January 2015 reported 84 percent of Americans "feel 'a lot' or

Strong passwords, antivirus software, and an awareness of cybercrime tactics can all help protect individual users from malicious hackers.

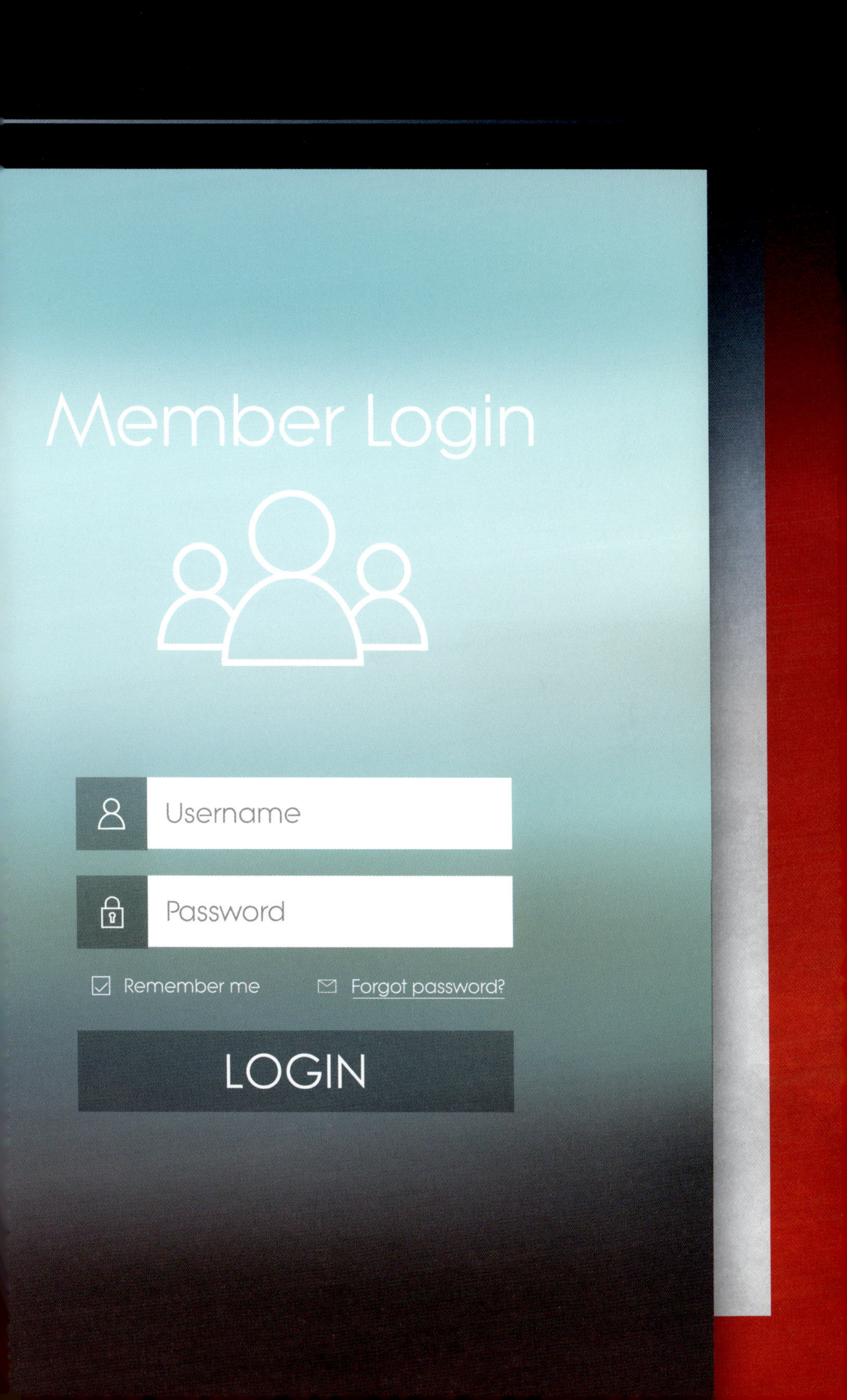
Member Login
Username
Password
Remember me
Forgot password?
LOGIN

a 'tremendous amount' of responsibility to protect their personal information."[1] One thing that keeps some people from employing cybersecurity measures is that they do not know exactly what is at stake in terms of how their information is being collected and how it is being used.

## HACKING INDIVIDUALS

Cybercriminals use a wide variety of tactics to infiltrate an individual's computer. Phishing, Trojan horses, and malicious downloads provide access to people's data. Unsecured wireless networks and the increasing integration of everyday appliances and utilities into the Internet can make these attacks more devastating than they would have been in the past.

### CYBERBULLYING

Cyberbullying, using the Internet to intimidate, harass, or cause harm, is a type of cyberthreat. Also called electronic aggression, it can be carried out by and targeted at people of any age, although increasing numbers of perpetrators and targets are adolescents. The Centers for Disease Control and Prevention reports between 9 and 35 percent of young people say they have been victims of electronic aggression.[2] As of early 2015, nearly 50 percent of US states included cyberbullying statutes.[3] Penalties ranged from school suspension and expulsion to jail time for criminal misdemeanors and felonies.

In common phishing attacks, an e-mail to the victim asks for help getting money out of a foreign country or

# MORE TO THE STORY

## COMBATTING E-MAIL FRAUD IN AUSTRALIA

Individual cyberthreats are a global problem. The Australian Competition and Consumer Commission reported in February 2015 that citizens lose $75,000 a day to online fraud.[4] Police attempting to combat cybercrimes originating outside Australia face the usual challenges of underreporting, working with foreign governments, and resolving issues of false or stolen identities. To overcome those challenges, several Australian police departments teamed up with the West Australian Department of Commerce to proactively combat cyberfraud by identifying individuals who were sending money to West African countries known for e-mail fraud.

Using this financial intelligence information, the Commerce Department sent letters to individuals who were sending money to those suspect countries. The letters stated the individuals might be victims of fraud and encouraged them to stop sending money. If an individual continued sending money, a second letter was sent enclosing a fact sheet for fraud victims. The project was considered a success. Approximately 66 percent of those receiving the first letter stopped payments, and 44 percent of second letter recipients stopped payments.[5] How those letter recipients felt about their financial information being used in this way by the police was not revealed.

tells the victim he or she has won a contest. Included in the e-mail is a request for the victim to send his or her bank account number, personal information, or money. In 2012, the FBI received thousands of reports of this type of incident, resulting in more than $55 million in total losses to victims.[6]

Opening an attachment on an e-mail can download a virus called a Trojan horse. One type of Trojan horse records everything the victim types and then sends it back to the hacker, giving the hacker access to usernames and passwords. Trojan horses are also used to make the

Phishing attacks use legitimate-looking e-mails to trick people into handing over personal information.

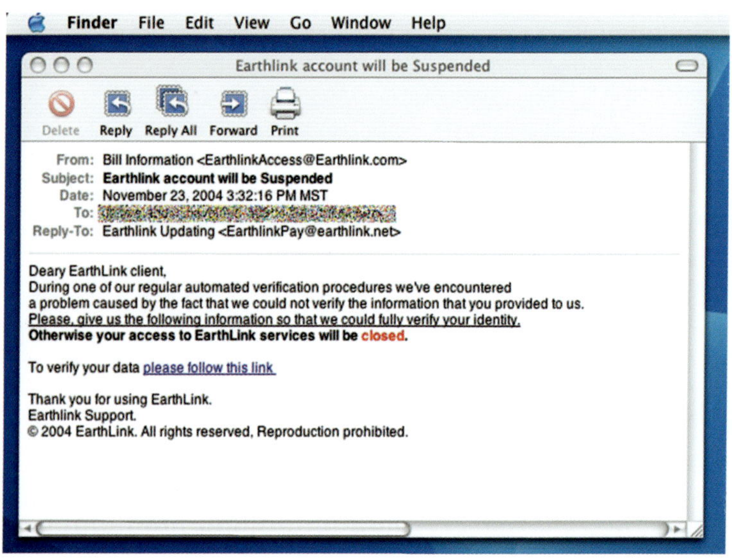

target computer part of a botnet. Ransomware is another example of a Trojan horse virus. Some computer programs have security weaknesses that can be used by hackers even if an individual uses security software on his or her computer. These weaknesses can be triggered when a malicious file downloads after a person intentionally clicks on a misleading link received via e-mail or social media.

## WHAT SHOULD VICTIMS DO?

Victims of cybercrime should report the incident to local law enforcement, the Internet Crime Complaint Center, the Federal Trade Commission, or a local group for victims of Internet crimes. These organizations have contact information online, and they can provide the victim with advice for steps to take.

Wireless networks, known as Wi-Fi networks, are commonly used within people's homes to permit Internet access to a variety of devices, such as smartphones, laptops, and streaming media devices. Wi-Fi networks can be secured with virtually unbreakable protections, but many users do not bother to secure their networks at all. Hackers can easily get into these unencrypted home networks and then break into people's computers. They can also target users who log on to public Wi-Fi networks, such as those at coffee shops or airports.

> "IF THIS WAS A TEST, MOBILE CONSUMERS WOULD BE FAILING. WHILE CONSUMERS ARE PROTECTING THEIR COMPUTERS, THERE IS A GENERAL LACK OF AWARENESS TO SAFEGUARD THEIR SMARTPHONES AND TABLETS. IT'S AS IF THEY HAVE ALARM SYSTEMS FOR THEIR HOMES, BUT THEY'RE LEAVING THEIR CARS UNLOCKED WITH THE WINDOWS WIDE OPEN."[8]
>
> **—MARIAN MERRITT, INTERNET SAFETY ADVOCATE FOR SYMANTEC CORPORATION**

The growing practice of connecting household devices and appliances to the Internet, including phones, coffee makers, thermostats, cars, refrigerators, and televisions, is one of the latest potential cybersecurity vulnerabilities. These devices often have few security features built in, making them ripe targets for hacking. Some have even been used in criminal botnets. According to an information technology research firm, there will be more than 26 billion Internet-connected devices by 2020. Governments and militaries are taking the smart-appliance threat seriously.[7]

## IDENTITY THEFT

Cybercriminals can use stolen credit cards to create new identities. Contacting the company that issued the card and using the victim's stolen password, the criminal can change the mailing address to his or her own. The criminal can then use the credit card to get a passport or driver's license, using his or her own photo but with the victim's name. Armed with these new forms of identification, the criminal can then open up bank accounts, apply for other credit cards, get a new social security card, and take out loans, all under the victim's name. This practice is known as identity theft.

Cybercriminals can similarly steal an individual's identity using a social security number, phone and utility account numbers, bank account numbers, college financial aid information, and driver's license numbers. All of this activity can occur without the victim knowing it is happening, until a bank or credit card company informs the victim that he or she has amassed huge, unpaid debts. Identity theft is an international problem and can take years for the victim to resolve.

## DATA MINING

Criminals are not the only hackers finding their way into individual computers. When Edward Snowden leaked thousands of secret NSA documents in 2013, members of the public were shocked to learn the intelligence agency had been conducting widespread surveillance on millions of Americans in the United States and abroad. It had done so by gathering records of e-mails and other online activity. Intelligence community supporters argued such surveillance was necessary to thwart terrorism, while privacy advocates believed surveillance without evidence of wrongdoing was illegal. Some reforms have been made in the way the US government gathers and keeps intelligence, though in 2015 the NSA was still allowed to gather data on Americans without a warrant.

"I THINK THE BIGGEST CONCERNS [ABOUT DATA MINING] ARE RELATED TO ORGANIZATIONS USING MY PERSONAL IDENTIFIABLE DATA, USAGE, AND STORAGE AGAINST ME."[9]

**—BILL SCHMARZO, CHIEF TECHNOLOGY OFFICER FOR EMC GLOBAL SERVICES**

Corporations also mine individual online data for more commercial reasons. Every time an Internet user clicks on a link, makes an online purchase, posts a message on social media, or uses an application on a mobile device, companies collect that information and use it to make general marketing decisions or target the consumer with individual

The NSA has used sophisticated data mining techniques in its surveillance programs.

advertising. This type of data mining is legal, though not everyone agrees it is ethical.

# FROM THE HEADLINES

## RANSOMWARE VICTIMS

In early 2015, a ransomware virus locked a Canadian couple's computer. They paid a cybercriminal $800 to unencrypt their computer so they could recover their small business records and photos of their kids and honeymoon. Even though the couple had backed up their data to an external hard drive, they had left the drive attached to the computer, so it, too, was locked by the encryption malware.

Ransomware infections are spreading rapidly, according to the security firm McAfee Labs, with a 155 percent increase during the last three months of 2014. Michelle Dennedy, chief privacy officer for Intel Security, estimates cybercriminals are making $10 to $50 million a month from ransomware.[10] Cybercriminals have expanded their targets from personal computers to businesses, governments, and cell phones.

The victimized couple noted they had done the right thing by backing up their hard drive, but they had made a huge mistake by not unplugging it, leaving it just as vulnerable to encryption

A piece of ransomware known as Blackshades struck computers across the world in 2014.

as their computer. If their external drive had remained safe, they could have gone to a computer store, had a technician remove the malware from their computer, and recovered all of their files from the external drive. With no available backups, though, they were forced to pay to get their data back.

CHAPTER SEVEN

# ELECTRONIC WARFARE AND TERROR

The military and civil-defense landscape has changed dramatically with the advent of the Internet. In the 1960s and 1970s, a spy might have snuck into a foreign government office, stolen a single paper file, and considered that a great success. Today, if cyberspies can break into a government computer network, they likely have access to thousands of secret files. Countries hire hackers to steal cutting-edge technology, interfere with another country's infrastructure, spy on dissidents, steal military plans, and remotely control enemy military equipment. While some experts disagree about the seriousness of

Director of National Intelligence James Clapper testified about cyberwarfare before the Senate Armed Services Committee in February 2015.

the issue—pointing out no one has yet been killed from a cyberattack—cyberincidents are on the rise.

## CYBERWAR INCIDENTS

In 2002, London hacker Gary McKinnon broke into US military computers looking for evidence of alien technology. Since then, the military has been trying to fix the vulnerabilities in its computer systems. In the years since, there have been multiple significant hacks related to national and international security.

### THE DEFINITION OF CYBERWAR

The North Atlantic Treaty Organization (NATO), a military alliance of North American and European countries, offers three conditions that must be met for a cyberattack to be considered an act of cyberwar. First, sensitive data must be leaked or stolen. Second, access to data is blocked, making it inaccessible to its owners. Third, a person dies as a result of the attack. NATO's first two conditions have occurred in the real world, but a case of the third has not yet been documented.

In 2005, China began a series of attacks on US government computers at the Department of Homeland Security, the Department of Defense, and other military departments, trying to steal classified information. Code-named Titan Rain, the cyberattacks by the Chinese army marked the beginning of an ongoing US cyberwar with China.

Two years later, in 2007, Estonian banks, news media, and government websites were crashed by a hacker protesting the dismantling of a World War II memorial. The cyberattack showed one person had the power to take down a country's vital infrastructure.

In 2008, the Conficker virus, which exploited security flaws in Microsoft Windows, infected millions of computers around the world within weeks. The malware connected infected computers into a huge botnet, capable of overpowering banking, communications, health care, and other vital computer networks.

Another attack came in 2009, when US officials revealed Russian and Chinese hackers had infiltrated US power grids, leaving behind software that could disrupt the utilities at the flick of a switch. The Chinese government denied the accusation. That same year, North Korea allegedly conducted days of ongoing cyberattacks against US government websites after the United States imposed sanctions on that country.

US companies came under cyberattack in 2010, when hackers located in China broke into Adobe, Symantec, Yahoo, Morgan Stanley, Northrop Grumman, and other corporations, stealing massive amounts of information. The stolen data included files about US surveillance targets, including data about Chinese spies being monitored in the United States. The hack was called Operation Aurora after the type of software the hackers used. That same year also brought the news of the Stuxnet malware's attack against an Iranian nuclear facility.

In 2011, cybersecurity firm McAfee uncovered an operation called Shady RAT, named for the remote administration tool the hackers used. It was a five-year span of attacks against 70 worldwide corporations, governments, and nonprofit organizations, including the International Olympic Committee. Though McAfee did not name those responsible for the hack, many observers believed it was the Chinese government. A variety of intellectual property was stolen.

Two significant cyberattacks took place in 2013. In May, the US Department of Defense reported hackers from China accessed plans for advanced US weapons

China denied accusations it had stolen plans for the F-35, though Edward Snowden released documents suggesting this was the case.

systems, including the Patriot missile and F-35 Joint Strike Fighter. Also in May, hackers with support from the Iranian government targeted US oil and gas companies.

In November 2014, the hacking of Sony Pictures led to the theft of employee information, e-mails, and thousands of documents. Following an investigation, the FBI linked the attack to North Korea.

## CYBERTERROR THREATS

Cyberterrorism is the use of attacks against computers or networks in order to cause harm or intimidate others. It might be carried out by countries, groups, or individuals wanting to further a social, ideological, religious, or political cause. It also might be done simply to cause havoc. The Stuxnet worm proved hackers could take command of mechanical systems and cause them to stop working. There are many other cyberterror targets that worry US and international governments alike.

Utilities are one of the largest potential targets. In 2013, the US Congress released a report revealing more than 12 US utility companies were under constant cyberattack. Speaking about the threat to utilities, US Secretary of Defense Leon Panetta said in 2012, "[Foreign cyberactors] are seeking to create advanced tools to attack these systems and cause panic, destruction and even loss of life."[1]

## CYBERATTACKS ON THE RISE

In 2012, the Department of Homeland Security reported 198 known attacks on critical infrastructure in the United States. That compares with only nine known attacks in 2009. The National Cybersecurity and Communications Integration Center reported 190,000 cyberincidents in fiscal year 2012, increasing to more than 214,000 the next year.[2] Thus far, the cyberintruders have only snooped, but government officials fear the hackers could return to carry out acts of sabotage.

Transportation systems are also vulnerable to attacks, posing a serious risk to human life. In 2008, a 14-year-old boy in the city of Lodz, Poland, used a homemade device that caused four trains to jump their tracks. Luckily, no one was killed. In 2011, hackers disrupted rail signals in the Pacific Northwest for two days. The next year, Panetta warned that "an aggressor nation or extremist group could gain control of critical switches and derail passenger trains, or trains loaded with lethal chemicals," resulting in a "cyber Pearl Harbor."[3]

Infrastructure, such as water plants, can also be hit by cybercrime. In 2011, hackers toggled the water pumps of an Illinois water plant off and on until one pump burned out. That same year, a hacker accessed a South Houston, Texas, water system that used a simple three-character password. The hacker wanted to prove how easy it was to do.

Even objects in space are not beyond the reach of dedicated hackers. Two US government satellites were hacked in 2007. An attack on satellites could cause a number of problems, including disrupting a nation's communications systems.

National economies can be dramatically impacted by relatively simple hacks. On April 23, 2013, hackers broke

## NO RULES

One of the factors complicating the new era of cyberwarfare is a lack of rules similar to those that govern conventional armed military combat. Some countries, including Russia and China, are pressing to implement international treaties as a way to control cyberactivity. Western countries, such as the United States and the United Kingdom, are wary of international treaties because they might require governments to reveal their true cyberwarfare capabilities.

into the Associated Press's Twitter feed and posted a fake news announcement saying President Obama had been injured in an attack on the White House. The tweet created a panic on Wall Street, resulting in a brief $200 billion drop in the stock market.[4]

## HOW REAL ARE THE THREATS?

Historical hacking incidents have proved damaging a nation's infrastructure is possible. But some privacy advocates believe the US government has overblown the possibility of serious cyberthreats in order to make the public more accepting of government oversight of the Internet. At a September 2013 Brookings Institution panel discussion, four cybersecurity experts agreed that even the worst current cyberattacks should be classified as espionage or sabotage, not acts of war. Cybersecurity expert Peter Singer believes there has been a lot of "hype and hysteria" about the subject.[5]

The impact the April 23, 2013, Twitter hack had on the stock market demonstrated how quickly malicious hackers can cause damage in the Internet age.

On the flip side of the debate, some cybersecurity experts say the threat is real and needs to be taken seriously. Jason Healey, a former White House cybersecurity aide, thinks as computer networks control more real machines—from generators to drones to entire homes—the risk increases for a cyberattack that will cause physical damage or even deaths. The interconnectedness of the Internet and the ability of hackers to remain anonymous make cyberattacks an enticing option for poorly funded terrorists and small countries with meager military capabilities. Information security specialist Dorothy Denning wrote, "While a vast majority of hackers may be disinclined towards violence, it would only take a few to turn cyber terrorism into reality."[6]

CHAPTER EIGHT

# DEFENSE AND OFFENSE

While a strong defense is key to protecting against cyberattacks, especially for individual users of the Internet, governments and corporations are also going on the offensive to improve cybersecurity. The US government has enacted laws to help prosecute cybercriminals and deter future attacks.

## US LAWS AND REGULATIONS

The hacking of state secrets and intelligence is a headache for the US government, whether it is done for fun or with malicious intent. The federal Computer Fraud and Abuse Act (CFAA), originally enacted in 1986, forbids unauthorized access to government computers. Punishments range from fines or probation for minor

For three decades, the US Congress has been passing legislation aimed at prosecuting cybercriminals.

SEN. PRYOR

offenses to 20 years in prison for more serious offenses. CFAA has been amended several times, most recently in 2008 with the Theft Enforcement and Restitution Act. This change makes it easier to prosecute cybercriminals and make them repay stolen money.

Prosecuting foreign cybercriminals has always been complicated, partly because hacking laws vary from one country to another. US law enforcement officials must petition countries to have suspects extradited, a process that can take years. In one such case, it took the United States five years—from 2002 to 2007—to finally extradite Gary McKinnon of the United Kingdom, who was accused of hacking into 97 US government computers.[1]

On April 1, 2015, President Obama issued an executive order declaring cyberattacks a national emergency. The order gives the US Department of the Treasury more power to impose economic sanctions against foreign nations who threaten critical infrastructure, launch denial-of-service attacks, or try to steal financial data or trade secrets. Even though computer crime experts consider the executive order long overdue, enforcing it will be difficult. It remains challenging to determine who

The US government accused McKinnon of causing hundreds of thousands of dollars in damage to its computer systems.

is responsible for a hack and whether the right person or country is actually being sanctioned. The executive order also does not address the role US companies play in being cybercrime victims by not better protecting their data. Nick Ackerman, an attorney and computer crime expert, told a reporter, "It should be a misdemeanor crime for companies not to take proper precautions."[2]

## CYBER DEFENSE VERSUS CYBER OFFENSE

Since the early days of the Internet, cybersecurity has largely been a matter of playing defense. Some cybersecurity experts call this the citadel approach, building a virtual fortress around data through the use of firewalls and data encryption. Firewalls filter network traffic by detecting suspicious patterns of programming code and preventing them from intruding into a computer network. Data encryption disguises information in a way that can only be decoded with the encryption key, which is known only to the sender and receiver of the message. Regardless of the defensive measures taken, computer networks are never 100 percent secure.

Given the problems of prosecuting foreign cybercriminals and the inability to keep networks completely safe, governments and militaries have placed more emphasis on offense. In a 2012 presidential policy directive, the Obama administration presented Offensive Cyber Effects Operations (OCEO), which could "offer unique and unconventional capabilities to advance US national objectives around the world with little or no warning to the adversary or target and with potential effects ranging from subtle to severely damaging."[3]

In March 2013, the Pentagon announced it was setting up as many as 100 cyber teams—both in the United States and in other countries—to carry out offensive cyberoperations to combat electronic threats against the United States. Those offensive operations might include blinding an enemy's radar or shutting down military command systems. In 2014, the US Air Force spent more than double on cyber offense what it did on cyber defense. The US Air Force specifies cyber offense as disrupting or eliminating the enemy's ability to use its computers and networks. The Department of Homeland Security and US intelligence agencies, such as the NSA and CIA, have also increased their cyber-offensive capabilities, including fighting the theft of trade secrets.

## CHARGES BUT NO ARRESTS

In a demonstration of how difficult it can be to prosecute foreign cybercriminals, in May 2014 the US Justice Department charged five Chinese hackers accused of working for the Chinese military. The hackers allegedly conducted cyberespionage against US corporations. However, since the hackers live in China and will likely never be extradited by the Chinese government, they are out of reach of the US justice system.

In retaliation for attacks, private companies also go on the offensive by following perpetrators back into their networks to retrieve stolen data and sometimes plant destructive malware. Reverse hacking, or "hacking back," is a felony crime in the United States—the same

"STARTING TODAY, WE'RE GIVING NOTICE TO THOSE WHO POSE SIGNIFICANT THREATS TO OUR SECURITY OR ECONOMY BY DAMAGING OUR CRUCIAL INFRASTRUCTURE, DISRUPTING OR HIJACKING OUR COMPUTER NETWORKS, OR STEALING THE TRADE SECRETS OF AMERICAN COMPANIES OR THE PERSONAL INFORMATION OF AMERICAN CITIZENS FOR PROFIT."[5]

**—US PRESIDENT BARACK OBAMA, APRIL 1, 2015**

as for any type of hacking—but some experts believe law enforcement is unlikely to detect or prosecute the behavior. Joel Reidenberg, a law professor at Fordham University, told an interviewer, "If the only organization that gets harmed is a number of criminals' computers, I don't think it would be of great interest to law enforcement."[4]

Nevertheless, cyber offense raises legal and ethical questions. For example, under what circumstances can a victim retaliate against a hack? Is the real perpetrator on the receiving end of the retaliatory attack, or is it the owner of an innocent hijacked computer?

## PROTECTING INDIVIDUAL COMPUTERS

Individuals are the weakest links in cybersecurity, whether using computers in homes, businesses, or government offices. Following simple guidelines, though, can dramatically improve defense against cyberattacks.

Passwords should be updated regularly and consist of a long mix of numbers, upper- and lowercase letters, and symbols. People should not use the same password for different accounts. If a login requires answering a security question, the user should make sure the answer cannot be found online through other means, such as a Facebook account.

Keeping software, browsers, and operating systems up-to-date is one of the easiest ways to secure personal information. Software developers frequently update their programs to fix newly discovered security holes.

Some programs, such as Tor, can prevent users' online activity from being tracked. Critics say such programs make it easier for criminals to carry out illegal acts online. However, it also allows dissidents living in countries under heavy censorship to organize and communicate. Privacy-seeking people living in relatively free nations also use antitracking software.

Some types of cyberattacks, such as ransomware, can leave a user's data inaccessible. For this reason, it is critical

Tor's logo is an onion, representing the many layers of routers each packet travels through in order to hide a person's online activity.

for people to frequently back up their information to a second hard drive. The backup should then be unplugged from the computer so a potential hacker cannot access it.

Finally, computer users can change their computing behavior to improve their personal cybersecurity even further. Attachments and links in e-mails or text messages should only be opened from known users who have not been hacked themselves. Applications and other files should only be downloaded from trusted sites.

# MORE TO THE STORY

## TOR: GOOD WEB, DARK WEB

Originally developed by the US Department of Defense to protect government communications, Tor is a volunteer-run nonprofit organization that creates a software tool to help users remain anonymous online. While using Tor, the packets a person sends and receives are randomly bounced through many different routers—provided by volunteers—until the message arrives at its destination. This makes online movements very difficult to track. This anonymous aspect of Tor is a huge asset to dissidents and human rights activists working in countries where web access is monitored or censored.

Tor's anonymity also makes it an ideal tool for criminals and black markets. With Tor, users can access what is known as the Darknet, a subsection of the Internet. Here, cybercriminals and malware authors advertise and sell their hacking services and goods, including stolen credit card data and malware programs. It is also a place where real-world criminals can purchase black-market items such as drugs and guns. Assassins even offer their services. The 2013 US government shutdown of one Darknet store, Silk Road, showed that Tor is not invincible to law enforcement. At the same time, the US government supports Tor's ability to promote free speech and seems reluctant to shut it down completely.

**CHAPTER** NINE

# FUTURE CYBERTHREATS **AND FUTURE SOLUTIONS**

New computer and network technologies continue evolving, bringing transformational changes to the ways corporations, individuals, and governments behave online. As criminals find new ways to use these new technologies, advances in cybersecurity will need to keep up.

## FIVE TRENDS IMPACTING CYBERSECURITY

Peter Singer and Allan Friedman, authors of the book *Cybersecurity and Cyberwar: What Everyone Needs to*

In recent years, cybersecurity has become a top priority for government and business leaders.

WHITEHOUSE.GOV
THE WHITE HOUSE
SUMMIT ON CYBERSECURITY
AND CONSUMER PROTECTION
WH.GOV
The President
John Hennessy

# MORE TO THE STORY

## THE CYBER-INDUSTRIAL COMPLEX

The US military is hiring an increasing number of private defense contractors to assist in its battle against cybercrime. It is a lucrative business. The Pentagon's annual cyber defense budget increased from $3.9 to $4.7 billion between 2013 and 2014. One defense contractor, Booz Allen Hamilton, was awarded a five-year, $5.6 billion project to protect military networks.[1] Former NSA director Mike McConnell heads the company's cyber division.

Along with increased spending have come concerns about what is called the cyber-industrial complex. Critics worry that the Pentagon and private defense contractors will try to raise the public's level of fear over cyberseurity to justify their big budgets. "If you're in the business of selling safeguards against cyberthreats, as many large firms are, you have an incentive to hype the threat," General Keith Aftergood, head of the US Cyber Command, said in an interview.[2] But Aftergood and others also point out that genuine threats exist and should be defended against. Between 2015 and 2017, the United States plans to increase the staffing of US Cyber Command from 900 to 4,900 employees.[3]

*Know*, identify five trends that will affect the future of cybersecurity. The first is cloud computing, the trend toward people storing their data on faraway servers and then accessing it on the Internet, rather than keeping data on their personal hard drives. Amazon.com, Apple, Google, and many other web companies use cloud computing. The US military also sees the benefit of the cloud. In 2013, US general Martin Dempsey expressed a desire for the US military to stop running 15,000 separate computer networks and instead use a single "joint information environment" in the cloud.[4]

In theory, the cloud brings added security. Rather than relying on users to take appropriate defensive measures with personal data, cloud computing companies can set up extensive defenses around their centralized servers. This puts the responsibility for data security in the hands of professional security engineers rather than individuals. However, there is the risk that if the server is hacked, many people's data could be compromised at once.

Another key trend is known as big data. This concept involves the collection and analysis of massive quantities of data in order to make decisions. For example, Netflix, a company that streams video over the Internet, gathers vast amounts of data about the preferences of individual users. It analyzes what actors, shows, and themes its viewers like. Then its production teams create new series that satisfy these known preferences. Likewise, the NSA uses big data, analyzing millions of e-mails, phone calls, and other communications to uncover security threats to the United States. No matter how secure data is, hackers will attempt to retrieve it.

Singer and Friedman also take note of the rapid rise of mobile devices connected to the Internet. The percentage of visitors to websites from smartphones and tablets increased from 1.6 percent in 2010 to 20.2 percent in 2012. New malware has followed these users to their new devices. By 2013, there were more than 350,000 unique examples of malware targeting mobile devices.[5] A few years earlier, there had been virtually none.

The shifting demographics of Internet users will also affect cybersecurity going forward. In 2000, the number of Internet users in North America and Asia were about equal. By 2014, there were four times more Internet users

With more Internet use moving to tablets, smartphones, and perhaps even watches, the future of cybersecurity will need to include protections for these mobile devices.

in Asia than in North America. Many other regions have also experienced huge increases in Internet access.

The Internet was originally based on the idea of sharing and openness. But many countries do not share those same ideals. Many nations, most notably China, heavily censor Internet access for their citizens. They block access to materials they deem offensive or challenging to the government. This raises the risk that the Internet may become divided, with governments walling off their own subsection of the Internet and limiting the public's access to information.

## SPYING FEARS

According to a Pew Research Center survey released on March 16, 2015, more than half of all Americans are worried about the US government spying on them, but few are doing anything about it. Most of those surveyed said either they do not know what security measures are available or they believe Internet spying is too difficult to avoid.

The final trend Singer and Friedman believe will have a significant effect on cybersecurity is the growing interconnectedness between computing devices and the real world—the Internet of Things. Even now, home thermostats and coffee pots can be controlled from mobile phones. Central computers control critical infrastructure and industrial machines. Delving deeply into personal networks can allow a hacker to learn when a family is away so he can burgle the house. Getting into corporate or governmental networks can let a criminal disrupt a major electrical grid. As protocols are developed that enable more devices to interact with each other, implementing security protections will be critical.

## FUTURE SOLUTIONS FOR CYBERSECURITY

A few people have suggested hacking today's networks is so easy that the entire Internet should be trashed and rebuilt from scratch with security in mind. But the pervasive presence of the modern Internet is so integral to individuals, businesses, and governments that starting over is not an option. Cybersecurity experts have recommended several solutions for keeping computers and data safe.

First, public education is critical. Most people who do not take security precautions with their personal computers and networks simply do not know how to take those precautions. Cybersecurity education is important for individual users and for anyone who operates and manages secure systems.

Another way to protect online assets is to create secure networks within the Internet for sensitive data and equipment, such as power grids. Experts who implement these networks must balance this approach with the benefits that the openness of the normal Internet provides.

## NO MORE PASSWORDS

People should use unique—and complicated—passwords for every website and application they use. But remembering all of those passwords can be difficult and frustrating. Different companies are exploring ways to get around remembering passwords. Sensors can unlock a smartphone upon recognizing a user's fingerprint. Users can draw patterns and images on touchscreens, rather than entering a password. Other new systems can identify users based on heartbeats and the irises of a person's eyes.

A 2015 exhibition in Israel gave cyber defense companies a chance to pitch their services to countries and corporations from around the world.

Governments have a role to play, too. They can develop or expand the international treaties that deal with Internet communications, hacking, and cybersecurity to standardize these efforts across different countries. Governments can also increase research funding to improve their knowledge of the latest cybersecurity threats. This research may also improve the ability of law enforcement agencies to easily and accurately determine the true culprits behind cyberattacks.

> "JUST AS WHEN AN INDIVIDUAL WHO IS NOT VACCINATED PUTS OTHERS' HEALTH AT RISK, COMPUTERS THAT ARE NOT PROTECTED OR HAVE BEEN COMPROMISED WITH A BOT PUT OTHERS AT RISK AND POSE A GREATER THREAT TO SOCIETY."[6]
>
> **—SCOTT CHARNEY, VICE PRESIDENT OF TRUSTWORTHY COMPUTING AT MICROSOFT**

Computer networks have made it easier than ever to use computers to learn, work, and play. The Internet, consisting of billions of interconnected computers around the world, is among the most significant technological developments in human history. However, this exciting new frontier has brought with it new dangers and risks. Motivated criminals are capable of using the Internet for personal gain or to carry out orders from an organization or government. In the future, they may even be able to use hacking to take human lives. Cybersecurity experts are working to deter them. As more people and devices connect to the Internet in the coming years, cybersecurity will continue growing in importance.

# ESSENTIAL FACTS

## MAJOR EVENTS

- In 1969, the first computer network, the ARPANET, is launched.
- The federal Computer Fraud and Abuse Act is passed by the US Congress in 1986, making tampering with computers a felony crime punishable by jail time and fines.
- In June 2010, cybersecurity analysts announce the discovery of the Stuxnet worm, the first known cyberweapon with the ability to damage real-world machines.
- On January 2, 2015, the United States imposes economic sanctions against North Korea in response to a cyberattack against Sony Pictures.

## KEY PLAYERS

- Tim Berners-Lee creates a hypertext language called HTML and is credited with being the inventor of the World Wide Web.

- Kevin Mitnick is a black-hat hacker who is convicted in 1999 and spends five years in prison. Upon his release, he works as a cybersecurity consultant.
- Edward Snowden leaks NSA documents about surveillance programs to journalists in June 2013.

## IMPACT ON SOCIETY

People have been hacking into computer software both out of curiosity and for personal gain since the advent of the Internet. Today, no individual, corporation, or government computer is completely immune from being infiltrated by hackers. These hackers may seek to steal money and secrets, spy on enemies, or wreak havoc on a nation's infrastructure or military capabilities. Cybercrime is on the rise and will continue to be a serious issue in the years to come. It is changing people's online behavior, making them wary of how they interact with the web and creating an entirely new cybersecurity industry.

## QUOTE

"It's the great irony of our Information Age—the very technologies that empower us to create and to build also empower those who would disrupt and destroy. . . . Cyber threat is one of the most serious economic and national security challenges we face as a nation."

*—President Barack Obama, May 29, 2009*

# GLOSSARY

**BREACH**
A break made in someone's defenses.

**CYBER**
Related to computers or computer technology.

**DISSIDENT**
A person who opposes official policy.

**ENCRYPT**
To disguise information to prevent access.

**ESPIONAGE**
Spying.

**EXTRADITE**
To hand over a suspected criminal to another nation.

**INFILTRATE**
To gain access in a secretive way.

**INFRASTRUCTURE**
The basic equipment and structures that are needed for a country, region, or organization to function properly.

**MALICIOUS**
Intending to do harm.

**OPERATING SYSTEM**
The software that supports a computer's basic functions.

**PERPETRATOR**
Someone who brings about or carries out a crime.

**PROTOCOL**
A system of rules.

**SABOTAGE**
To deliberately destroy, damage, or obstruct something, especially for military or political advantage.

**SANCTION**
Threatened penalty for disobeying a law or rule.

**SURVEILLANCE**
Close observation.

**VULNERABILITY**
Something susceptible to attack or harm.

# ADDITIONAL RESOURCES

## SELECTED BIBLIOGRAPHY

Kushner, David. "The Geeks on the Front Lines: The Battle between Government and Industry for America's Best Hackers." *Rolling Stone*. Rolling Stone, Sept. 2013. Web. 3 Mar. 2015.

Seabrook, John. "Network Insecurity." *The New Yorker*. The New Yorker, 20 May 2013. Web. 3 Mar. 2015.

Singer, P. W., and Allan Friedman. *Cybersecurity and Cyberwar: What Everyone Needs to Know*. New York: Oxford UP, 2014. Print.

## FURTHER READINGS

Espejo, Roman. *Policing the Internet*. Farmington Hills, MI: Greenhaven, 2012. Print.

Mitnick, Kevin, and William L. Simon. *Ghost in the Wires: My Adventures as the World's Most Wanted Hacker*. New York: Little Brown, 2011. Print.

## WEBSITES

To learn more about Special Reports, visit **booklinks.abdopublishing.com**. These links are routinely monitored and updated to provide the most current information available.

## FOR MORE INFORMATION

For more information on this subject, contact or visit the following organizations:

Computer History Museum
1401 North Shoreline Boulevard
Mountain View, CA 94043
650-810-1010
http://www.computerhistory.org

The Computer History Museum houses the world's largest collection of computer hardware, software, and other material related to the history of computing, including the birth of the Internet and cybersecurity.

US Department of Defense
1400 Defense Pentagon
Washington, DC 20301
703-571-3343
http://www.defense.gov/home/features/2013/0713_cyberdomain

The US Department of Defense (DoD) is home to US Cyber Command, which focuses on securing cyberspace for military command and control. Public tours of the Pentagon are allowed with advance reservations.

# SOURCE NOTES


## CHAPTER 1. THE WORM THAT CHANGED THE CYBER WORLD

1. Sharon Weinberger. "Computer Security: Is This the Start of Cyberwarfare?" *Nature*. Nature, 8 June 2011. Web. 5 May 2015.

2. Ibid.

3. P. W. Singer and Allan Friedman. *Cybersecurity and Cyberwar: What Everyone Needs to Know*. New York: Oxford UP, 2014. Print. 2.

4. Ibid. 60.

5. "Fact Sheet: Cybersecurity Legislative Proposal." *White House*. White House, 12 May 2011. Web. 7 Mar. 2015.

6. John Seabrook. "Network Insecurity." *New Yorker*. New Yorker, 20 May 2013. Web. 3 Mar. 2015.

7. P. W. Singer and Allan Friedman. *Cybersecurity and Cyberwar: What Everyone Needs to Know*. New York: Oxford UP, 2014. Print. 2.

## CHAPTER 2. INTERNET HISTORY

1. Kenneth Geers. "Strategic Cyber Security." *NATO*. NATO, June 2011. Web. 3 Mar. 2015.

2. Mary Bellis. "Inventors of the Modern Computer: ARPAnet—The First Internet." *About.com*. About.com, n.d. Web. 8 Mar. 2015.

## CHAPTER 3. HOW IT ALL WORKS

1. Roger Johnston. "How I Hacked an Electronic Voting Machine." *Popular Science*. Popular Science, 5 Nov. 2012. Web. 23 June 2015.

2. "Did You Visit HuffPo Last Week? You Might Have a Virus." *CNN*. CNN, 8 Jan. 2015. Web. 8 Apr. 2015.

## CHAPTER 4. HACKERS AND HACKTIVISTS

1. David Kushner. "The Geeks on the Front Lines: The Battle Between Government and Industry for America's Best Hackers." *Rolling Stone*. Rolling Stone, Sept. 2013. Web. 3 Mar. 2015.

2. Martin C. Libicki, David Senty, and Julia Pollak. "Hackers Wanted." *RAND*. RAND, 2014. Web. 23 June 2015.

3. Lee Munson. "What Are the Main Differences between Hackers and Crackers?" *Security-FAQs*. Security-FAQs, 9 Mar. 2013. Web. 23 June 2015.

4. Raf Sanchez. "WikiLeaks Q & A: Who Is Bradley Manning and What Did He Do?" *Telegraph*. Telegraph, 30 July 2013. Web. 23 June 2015.

5. "Snowden and the Debate on Surveillance Versus Privacy." *Reuters Institute for the Study of Journalism*. University of Oxford, 16 Dec. 2014. Web. 23 June 2015.

## CHAPTER 5. THREATS TO COMPANIES

1. Michael Riley, Ben Elgin, Dune Lawrence, and Carol Matlack. "Missed Alarms and 40 Million Stolen Credit Card Numbers: How Target Blew It." *Bloomberg Business*. Bloomberg, 13 Mar. 2014. Web. 23 June 2015.

2. Ibid.

3. Hiroko Tabuchi. "$10 Million Settlement in Target Data Breach Gets Preliminary Approval." *New York Times*. New York Times, 19 Mar. 2015. Web. 1 Apr. 2015.

4. "Target Appoints New Chief Information Officer, Outlines Updates on Security Enhancements." *Target*. Target, 29 Apr. 2014. Web. 23 June 2015.

5. Lisa Richwine. "Cyber Attack Could Cost Sony Studio as Much as $100 Million." *Reuters*. Reuters, 9 Dec. 2014. Web. 23 June 2015.

6. Ben Elgin and Michael Riley. "Now at the Sands Casino: An Iranian Hacker in Every Server." *Bloomberg Business*. Bloomberg, 11 Dec. 2014. Web. 23 June 2015.

7. Damian Paletta. "FBI Official: No Evidence Sony Hack Was Inside Job." *Wall Street Journal*. Wall Street Journal, 8 Jan. 2015. Web. 13 Mar. 2015.

8. Dan Roberts. "Obama Imposes New Sanctions against North Korea in Response to Sony Hack." *Guardian*. Guardian, 2 Jan. 2015. Web. 2 Apr. 2015.

9. Ellen Nakashima. "Why the Sony Hack Drew an Unprecedented US Response against North Korea." *Washington Post*. Washington Post, 15 Jan. 2015. Web. 9 Apr. 2015.

10. Taylor Armerding. "The 15 Worst Data Security Breaches in the 21st Century." *CSO*. CSO, 15 Feb. 2012. Web. 2 Apr. 2015.

11. Ibid.

12. Ibid.

13. Sharone Tobias. "2014: The Year in Cyberattacks." *Newsweek*. Newsweek, 31 Dec. 2014. Web. 2 Apr. 2015.

14. Ibid.

15. Alyssa Newcomb. "Anthem Hack May Have Impacted Millions of Non-Customers as Well." *ABC News*. ABC News, 25 Feb. 2015. Web. 2 Apr. 2015.

# SOURCE NOTES CONTINUED

16. "Data-Breach Costs Take Toll on Target Profit." *CBS News*. CBS News, 26 Feb. 2014. Web. 2 Apr. 2015.

17. P. W. Singer and Allan Friedman. *Cybersecurity and Cyberwar: What Everyone Needs to Know*. New York: Oxford UP, 2014. Print. 228–230.

18. Mary Thompson. "Why Cyber-Insurance Will Be the Next Big Thing." *CNBC*. CNBC, 1 July 2014. Web. 27 Mar. 2015.

19. P. W. Singer and Allan Friedman. *Cybersecurity and Cyberwar: What Everyone Needs to Know*. New York: Oxford UP, 2014. Print. 89.

## CHAPTER 6. THREATS TO PERSONAL COMPUTERS

1. "Perceptions of Privacy Online and in the Digitally Connected World." *National Cybersecurity Alliance*. National Cybersecurity Alliance, 28 Jan. 2015. Web. 23 June 2015.

2. "Technology and Youth: Protecting Your Child From Electronic Aggression." *CDC*. CDC, n.d. Web. 1 Apr. 2015.

3. "Cyberbullying." *Findlaw*. Findlaw, n.d. Web. 1 Apr. 2015.

4. "Australians Lose $75,000 Every Day to Romance Scams." *ACCC*. ACCC, 15 Feb. 2015. Web. 6 May 2015.

5. Cassandra Cross. "How to Tackle Cyber Crime before People Even Know They're a Victim." *Phys.org*. Phys.org, 19 Mar. 2015. Web. 27 Mar. 2015.

6. Erika Eichelberger. "What I Learned Hanging Out with Nigerian Email Scammers." *Mother Jones*. Mother Jones, 20 Mar. 2014. Web. 30 Mar. 2015.

7. Jacob Morgan. "A Simple Explanation of 'The Internet of Things.'" *Forbes*. Forbes, 13 May 2014. Web. 31 Mar. 2015.

8. "2013 Norton Report: Cost per Cybercrime Victim up 50 Percent." *Symantec*. Symantec, 1 Oct. 2013. Web. 27 Mar. 2015.

9. Ellen Rooney Martin. "The Ethics of Big Data." *Forbes*. Forbes, 27 Mar. 2014. Web. 3 Apr. 2015.

10. David Common. "Ransomware Victims Pay Cybercriminals to Save Family Photos." *CBC*. CBC, 11 Mar. 2015. Web. 27 Mar. 2015.

## CHAPTER 7. ELECTRONIC WARFARE AND TERROR

1. John Seabrook. "Network Insecurity." *New Yorker*. New Yorker, 20 May 2013. Web. 3 Mar. 2015.

2. Ibid.

3. Ibid.

4. Tom Lauricella, Christopher S. Stewart, and Shira Ovide. "Twitter Hoax Sparks Swift Stock Swoon." *Wall Street Journal*. Wall Street Journal, 23 Apr. 2013. Web. 23 June 2015.

5. Sydney J. Freedberg Jr. "'Cyberwar' Is Over Hyped: It Ain't War Til Someone Dies." *Breaking Defense*. Breaking Defense, 10 Sept. 2013. Web. 23 June 2015.

6. Hossein Bidgoli, ed. *The Internet Encyclopedia, Vol. 1*. Hoboken, NJ: Wiley, 2004. Print. 361.

## CHAPTER 8. DEFENSE AND OFFENSE

1. "UK Hacker Loses Extradition Fight." *BBC News*. BBC, 3 Apr. 2007. Web. 18 Mar. 2015.

2. John Eggerton. "President Declares Cyber Attacks 'National Emergency.'" *Broadcasting and Cable*. Broadcasting and Cable, 1 Apr. 2015. Web. 3 Apr. 2015.

3. Glenn Greenwald and Ewen MacAskill. "Obama Orders US to Draw Up Overseas Target List for Cyber-Attacks." *Guardian*. Guardian, 7 June 2013. Web. 6 May 2015.

4. Scott Cohn. "Companies Battle Cyberattacks Using 'Hack Back.'" *CNBC*. CNBC, 4 June 2013. Web. 6 May 2015.

5. "Obama Signs Order Creating New Cyber Sanctions Program." *Huffington Post*. Huffington Post, 2 Apr. 2015. Web. 6 Apr. 2015.

## CHAPTER 9. FUTURE CYBERTHREATS AND FUTURE SOLUTIONS

1. Anna Mulrine. "Cyber Security: The New Arms Race for a New Front Line." *Christian Science Monitor*. Christian Science Monitor, 15 Sept. 2013. Web. 23 June 2015.

2. Ibid.

3. Ibid.

4. Vangie Beal. "Cloud Computing (The Cloud)." *Webopedia*. Webopedia, n.d. Web. 13 Mar. 2015.

5. P. W. Singer and Allan Friedman. *Cybersecurity and Cyberwar: What Everyone Needs to Know*. New York: Oxford UP, 2014. Print. 251.

6. Ibid. 177.

# INDEX

# ABOUT THE **AUTHORS**

Melissa Higgins writes fiction and nonfiction for children and young adults. Two of her novels for struggling readers, *Bi-Normal* and *I'm Just Me*, won silver medals in the Independent Publisher (IPPY) Book Awards. Higgins's nearly 40 nonfiction titles range from character development and psychology to history and biographies. When not writing, Higgins enjoys hiking and taking photographs around her home in the Arizona desert.

Michael Regan, MEd, worked for 30 years as a middle-school and college counselor and adviser before turning his attention to research and writing. He's especially interested in topics related to technology and current events. He lives in the Southwest.